The Kangaroo Farm

Martin Harrison

The Kangaroo Farm

Shearsman Library

Second Edition
Published in the United Kingdom in 2020 by
Shearsman Library
an imprint of Shearsman Books
by Shearsman Books Ltd
PO Box 4239
Swindon
SN3 9FN

Shearsman Books Ltd Registered Office
30–31 St. James Place, Mangotsfield, Bristol BS16 9JB
(this address not for correspondence)

www.shearsman.com

ISBN 978-1-84861-701-8

First published by Paper Bark Press, Brooklyn, NSW, Australia, 1997.
This new edition is published by kind permission of
the author's Estate and of Paper Bark Press.

CONTENTS

The Kangaroo Farm

Moon Gazing in Sorrento Dusk

Fire

Author's acknowledgements

Island, Ulitarra, Overland, Heat, Poetry (Chicago,) *Terra Australis,* and *The New World Tattoo: The 1996 Newcastle Poetry Prize Anthology* where a number of these poems appeared previously. For their advice and intuition, I would like to thank Ken Cruickshank, Marcia Stewart, Alexandra Buchler, Michael Hulse, Juno Gemes and Robert Adamson. Mrs Neilma Gantner and the Myer Foundation gave me invaluable breathing space for new writing in 1992. My thanks, too, to the Literature Board of the Australia Council for a fellowship in 1993, and to Mrs Lorri Whiting and the Australia Council for a residency in the B.R. Whiting Library, Rome, in 1995, where many of the poems were completed. Though late in the day it was there that I understood Pasolini's line, "Felice te, a cui il vento primaverile sa di vita..."

The book as a whole is dedicated to my sister, Barbara Lewis.

The Kangaroo Farm

Eels

The mythos of peninsular light
is that it drifts rich as snow,
or turns itself to creamy rivers
of cloudy sun in dusk-splashed trees.

Mornington winter sunset is
a dove in lift off through orange air,
glimpsed as you pass these well-stocked farms
whose wind breaks move like fleeing deer.

Sudden clearness happens in this winter fire,
brightening cold mist and diamond rain,
where a thing is placed, bird-like,
in the windscreen's single, whistling glance.

Myth gets us nowhere. The past is
the past's dream, the mind's water-fringe:
lost, dead tracks, eel-trap creeks,
the intent posture, flames leaping.

Red Tulips
for Ken

It's only accidental things you just don't joke about:
earlier, for instance, my sister phones about a death in Israel,
the ABC announces floods upstream along the Clarence,
and there was that sense of starting-up after a night's drunk
with hard flat squints of dazzlement at morning light
on a far off hill-line, snow-like, back of Surfers.
It's only scholarship will give them form and figure.

Last night, the host showed us the purple candelabra,
next, Spanish furniture in the pool-side dining-room:
we trailed past bull-hide seats, happy to barbecue.
Despite the purples, talk was funny – on books and history.
Falling for it, the white South African bowled wide and long,
till we moved to verities of wine and weather, then
on to regional style – finally, again, the role of scholars.

It's what you said. You take the book outside, settle down,
and find that flies and sudden wind and water change it all –
impossible, that is, to read, take notes, think out the piece.
The Spanish writers had this problem, too, with their siesta:
the day's whole pattern suited only shorter fiction
whereas big work came, ice-hard, from the North's refrigerator
of Alpine places, cold castles, among a blue-eyed *Kultur*:

I too would be an indoors lover and an outdoors hater
(with the minor reservation that I love to drive)
sheltering a life-long project built from imagined pasts,
querulous over details from the pre-Settler period,
Cavafy-like translating fragments into innovative metre
where a green-plush library invites me to sleep and work.
On this reckoning, Canberra's the place to head for.

Today, though, I wake in a high-rise overlooking the Pacific.
Mid-morning ocean's a blue wedge over a useless balcony.
Outside, the beach curves northwards like a horse's mane –
sand-dunes have the same soft bristles, the land's a neck –
till one of the tropics' five minute clouds, quick as a space-ship,
blots out the sun making a reef of moody mountain-dusk,
and the water-lines ripple like an untuned TV monitor:

it gives me a headache. It's a mid-tone most dinner guests like,
a patch where you needn't think past land and nation:
working them out through a confessional mode,
putting you in a given spot. There's a story here
of time told in anecdotes, sans the wit of the bush yarn's flukes,
becoming the first book, and the next, and the one which sinks:
student poets react against this, copying Duggan and Tranter.

To write, you need the cleanest light, one overcoming sense,
something to do with returns from a half-thought-out border,
instinctive but not without the shape of a sharp, dry mind,
(reading it, will that famous reviewer finally stop her gush?)
with wide plains detailed in a zoom, yet taken at a glance.
It's why, tidying up and sensing my mood, you place that pot
of exotics, the Tasmanian flame-tulips, on the balcony floor

past which the waves clash in a Dame Edna of gladioli storms
and the sea-dazzle becomes a wall of burnt-out stripes,
provoking this recall of past and present, of light in dark:
a twisted, woollen blue fragrance of the long-lost scarf,
memory of blue glass around a once-glimpsed shark fin,
a sense of radiance at the base of camel-humped clouds –
this and more, caught on a red edge, both ways from the shore.

Poetry and Paperbarks

for Kieran Condell

All down the street, paperbarks strip off their long brown swathes.
Stunted lifters of pavements, peeling crevices for moths,
the Harbour's wet grey dusk reaches them, piercing their clothes.

The light's familiar on them, but I wonder why they planted
them at the back of King's Cross, sheepish and huddled,
where restaurant-goers park their cars. On the corner, somewhere Thai.

They thrust out branches red as a desert's sunset pillars. I've seen
this red glow on them, mirrored in flood-water at Myall Lake,
as visions of dangling rags and fiery wood above a brackish sheen.

Pushy, they're chopped back down by city workers.
Along the gutter, roots shake earthquake tremors through tarmac.
Up top, they're pruned into sky-holes for power lines, their sides shaved
                for cars.

Dappled paperbarks, they're out of place in this phased-out dusk:
making an oasis for a passing glance,
they trace an underground watercourse in the earth's dry dark.

Like remnants at a paddock's edge, they fringe the Cross's swamp.
They greet me as I turn the corner looking for the place we meet.
It's the bark-effect which strikes me, that damp, unfolded wrapping-paper

with ham-fisted waxy leaves sprayed in air. I can't ignore them,
knowing how, for weeks, they'll distract me with their oddity.
Traditional, bush-verse paperbarks they speak a country theme

mixed up with axe-talk and the city's view of their soft, burnt filo.
In Melbourne they'd dig them up to put in flickering London planes.
For a second, they're contrast with the horizon's bone-white halo

like I was out at Hay a few days back, or finding the Murrumbidgee
ditched beneath the plain, winding south-westerly
in its dotted nature strip of dusty trees. Not quite paperbarks, it's true,

but with this same impact, this same sense that after arid space
you must once again look at sky through trees.
Through paperbarks even a clustered street is anchored in the mind.

Now tufted, underwaterlike, they catch the last sun's greenish splash.
Really, they're unimaginable, hard to place,
flourishing with no model apart from National Parks. As if to say:

you must not lose your local touch, specific to how your senses work.
True, some Australians still live in imported European fantasy,
and we've writers who'd rather live in yesterday's New York.

I too use images as linear as TV's and don't insist upon the past
or on the way the land intrudes its myths of ownership,
but you must not lose the way time floats ancestrally into your eyes

just because it's November, or just because an ocean of flashy evening,
polluted and unstable, gives off a whiff of Jakarta-style haze.
It's now familiarity. It's old light breeding invisible, touchable things.

Clouds Near Waddi

On looking up at the elephants
you could wonder where you were.
They were hovering on a chain
like Hannibal's in the Alps:

elephant shapes, bulging, linked together
crossing from north to south,
visible as a desert fantasy
of warnings, pillars, God's truth.

White narcissi, they came from nowhere
along the edge like sky's debris,
intruders in another medium
like stage scenery painted on that blue,

painted so you forgot Springtime hordes
of yellow daisies conquering new wheat,
or Paterson's Curse in purple ribbons
flickering either side of the road

and forgot those huge Egyptian prows
unmoored, two days back, amid green –
the Grampians, Mount Arapiles
drifting on the Wimmera's plain.

As I drove, earth was paradox,
flat for miles yet curving into clouds –
sensed like a rear-view mirror's glimpse
yet always opening up, leading onwards,

through skylines' endless replacements
which fixed each farm's chequerboards,
with Time measured in gum-tree tops
floating backwards on far horizons.

Saintliness

Like saints, they're clichés. They pass. They're moods.
Poets, like analysts, make money out of them, though
they're also how novelists set characters in a scene.
No-one quite expresses the mood, no-one talks of it.
But the whole action takes it on, dramatic,
lucid, full of those undercurrents like hidden threads
which make for richness. It's the classic moment:
war veteran at the small town's obelisk. Not a poem,

it's a moment so complex you'd rather forget it,
there's more there than you could possibly write.
No single image holds sky and earth together.
Wordless, it tears you apart. It's a blade of grass
picked out in the paddock. It's a sort of madness.
It's the blades of black swan's wings on shining water,
a bulky fragment floating where you loitered
watching time go by: yes, in that *sepulcrum*

mortis of what was fair or good, of what should have
worked out or of what X did to Y. No-one imagined
it. No-one could have thought it would be so bad.
All this occurs like a speck, a flash of light caught
on something bright, unmemorable, half-thought,
already swirled away like a red leaf in a run-off,
knocking you over in a thousand moving waves –
words, thoughts, laments. Thus: you've been forgotten.

Or: you're very old, go into town from time to time.
You've had the same neighbours now for years.
The lawyer phones sometimes to modify the will,
most often, though, to chat about poor winter-rain
and how the town's sinking without the train.
You wonder about those arty folks just up the line,
building their sheds without a permit. The Symes
would spin in their graves to see their orchard gone.

Each mood's a scene. Things don't change they just disappear,
like a street one side of which is taken down.
A vast white skyline stretches behind a scrubby fence
and who can tell the distance now in "everything"
in "no-one" "now" and "all?" Age is perving.
It's about the mind's long journey and your fears
of frailty. It's about sunlight on the kitchen table: years
of taking its Eucharist...... So it goes. On and on.

Even chattery moods erect their marble tombs.
Saints spin around in them like whirring dynamos.
Other moods fix the attention like frosted glass:
the restless mood, the angry mood, the mood
in which you wonder if you've ever been loved –
everyone knows that peevish sense of longing –
the mood where sounds occur just beneath hearing,
like heavy blue clouds behind a lemon-tree in a yard

in an old city you've dreamed about but never seen.
Like someone phoning round to say goodbye
moods make themselves known before they fly away:
till a moment arrives where all their torture ends,
all their rearing and pulling like horses, all the bent
backs straining, all their earthquakes under your words.
as if a voice breaking the billowing rococo shrouds
says This now is what you must do. So you do it.

Close-Ups

1. Sydney Harbour

Like the inside covers of an old book,
daybreak's grey sky has yellow marbled patches,
faint orange shades, luminous spaces over cumulus hills,
dizzying billow-shapes which could be steam-engine smoke,
together with down-hanging pothooks which could be bristles
of gulls' wings, or dangling pelican throats, or wind-taut sails
against icy wastes of flat cloud-shelf which Eskimos hunt across –
and, through everything, a slow blossoming of winter sea-light
where ocean water gleams like a hallway's polished floor. No old book,

it's a 7 a.m. July daybreak sky. Everything about childhood
has been floating about in my pre-dawn sleep. Waking just now,
there's a dream-trace of the moment in the cavalcade
of army trucks speeding down a wide, dusty boulevard
in a city I have never been to: the same trees grow in Manila,
the buildings a mix of high-rise and tin-roof. It's a mindscape.
It's a flash caught in the flesh, something held over when you drowse.
The truck I'm on is strobed under a palm-tree branch's shadow.
The air's heavy like Bangkok's. We're heading to the President's Palace

or to a temple. Giving it a name breaks it off. If it re-surfaces,
it'll be like a fish's back suddenly emerging from the water.
Or it's light catching a wave far out. The mind's paintbox
will paint it over. Dream-TV cables it underground. Its fading colours
blend with the daybreak's fire. We know the nerves work faster
than the conscious mind, blocking pain, sending a reflex,
making connections learnt in childhood where adult minds wisely pause:
nerves link what they transmit. But is it possible (between sky, dream and
        harbour-light) to think
this depthless gap? Marbled paper makes the leap. Adults like parachutists
        step from the plane.

2. Roadside Near Hillston

A crow on a fence-post in winter light
sets its acute on a mile of fence.
The driver passing on the red dirt road

focuses flatness on that black event –
its neck and dead-still beak, its indecision
whether to stay or not. The crow

is looking round, about to turn,
about to take off, leaping
an invisible ladder up to cirrus blue.

To tangible, wind-scalloped blue. It's not making
heavy weather out of landing here.
It can float up and take us all in –

take us as part of the land's glare –
as easily as wait and watch us
sailing by. Like a small detail at the side

of a Renaissance picture, it proves that even crows
are fruitful. This one flutters up,
settles again a few yards off. The kangaroo-bar, the rear-side

door, the crackling CB radio, slide past:
pebble-light, flashing in the road, bounces on our eyes.
Behind us, a pillar of smoke, a trail of dust.

Grass Parrot

Two days later, I see again
long hectares of white plains bristling
the other side of the road's verge:
blue marks flitter, opal showers flash,
becoming grass-parrots which leap up
from bleached waist-high grass, then back again
in tiny rocking-horse movements
of springing curves and perfect falls.
Foraging, they twitter a hundred miles.
Out there, heat-blurred across paddock glare,
dark trees float along the horizon's line:
bushes are wallabies, swivelling their ears.
Through my hair, hot wind's flooded creek.

Cloudless sky moves, without seeming to,
in an eye-blink over the Silver City Highway.

Tasmanian Tiger

for Neilma Gantner

To spend a year, at work, capturing a detail
of mist in winter she-oaks and a background
of lucid water glittering through turquoise dusk
in a sitting-room quiet as its fire-warm dark,
working out how the detail stays in mind
and why it does not fit the repertoire

of how to track a thing in wing-beats over time,
and why the magpie flaps up outside, steadying the mood
an which it is beheld, objectifying itself
by drawing edges which the eye cannot pass
even in whirring flocks of buck-white words;
skeins of similes for how things move far off,

is to be wakeful to a prompt given only once
whether drowned against the cloud-line's light,
or fixed as a move between two thoughts
about dim stag-horn shapes and back-lit mauves,
till they distract you from a wire brush's fans sprayed
closely on the window, midway up the nearest branch:

she-oak needles outside, that is, with the fineness
of a prisoner's diamond scratchmarks over glass,
forest-needles of a dense Norwegian night,
watchful and warning claws which do not flower
but seed from their own bud-like, myriad spurs
out into open, lake-mirroring attitudes

against mother-of-pearl-with-cloud dusk-light,
all banked up, echoing with wattlebirds and rain,
vestigial traces criss-crossing ice-white skies
like fibres, magnified, seen through a lens,
which seem to part, then swirl again
into motionless, hazy storms at each bough's end.

In weather like Tasmania's, the detail gives itself back.
It's taken a year to see how it keeps occurring there,
down rainbow-flickering shores of she-oak trees,
as something repetitive, caught again and again,
so drained of colour in sunset's orange-blossom glare
that, really to see it, you'd change a whole life's path:

ungraspable fineness of dark she-oak needles,
ungraspable, I think, because so fine,
a thing merely visual, meant only in passing
to an observer perplexed by see-through shadowiness,
focused in a consciousness of time
which freezes now in snowy blurs, then leaps out –

the bush's only tiger, sharp-fanged, springing,
in an image that's sublime, immaculately shot,
setting transparence in oily green-glazed water,
settling blackness in a guarded silhouette,
allowing, at a glance, the past to turn out right:
a museum exhibit, extinct, colourful, symbolic.

Icons

1. Prodigal Son

He walked in from the afternoon light.
Outside old grass shone in late sun's haze.
Bare earth by the sheep pens was oyster-silk,
cloudy river-swirl, a scuff of hoof-marks. He hadn't
thought it would come to this, a return

to somewhere where most things had changed.
The place still ran sheep and these days goats,
though last winter's rain had failed. New shoots were thin.
There was the house, the car, the school bus. There
was still money in the place. More to earn.

Some folk further north hadn't planted. Machinery
was for sale. Here a few dams still had murky eyes,
the creek dribbled from pool to pool. You could
cut wood from out of the valley's end. Out west,
they planned to drain a lake and truck it to cotton-

farmers, stuck in the drought. Thirty thousand for a wetland.
Most like, if the banks held off, you could make
a kind of life, with the wife working in a shop
in town. The wattle out the back had given up
its yellow, a previous owner's jacaranda soon

would burst its sky blue hair, watering that blue
upwards from the earth. These things hadn't changed.
You could go on. But only, if seeing past your past,
hardship and lack became simplicity: a sunset's
corrugated iron over desert. Unblind, he saw the place again.

2. Return Visit

He thinks of his daughter, as if she's already waiting
at the customs', thousands of miles to the east,
where glassy purples mass against the clouds' Arctics.
Way off in the future, she's just got into her car.
He wakes, settles back, cramped and uncomfortable:
in front, the boredom of books, head-sets, magazines,
reminding him of Bangkok's stinking water markets,
tinted ovals of hills, yellow with gorse, seen from coaches,
other planes arriving over snow-capped Alps,
fragments of school-boy French at a flower stall,
unknown memories he will have to find words for.
Perhaps photographs will absolve him from talk.
If they're memories, he waits to give them away,
as if he could now (flying home) shrink them down
into a snail-fossil dream, there smoothly crushed,
wrapped in his clothes, totally private, duty free.
In his sleep, they're frozen in leaves of eroded stone.
These are widowed thoughts, his life's scrapings,
nothings which resume him and his long-lost childhood,
glimpses as eel-glittering as Scottish lochs.
Nothing so still as mid-point in a creek in flood.
He sees a crazy pencil racing down a page:
it's the jumbo jet's shadow as it tracks
through its imaginary waste of cold, thin air.
It's held on its curve. It's a thought in the sun.
Dumb, mute, the symbols he carries fit the light,
like fallen fruit, busied by wasps, beneath an orchard tree.
Far below, dry rivers are cracks mapping a canyon.
Sideways, a three hour sunset abandons the desert
so that, by now, it seems he's flying another planet
under a blood-streaked bonfire of oncoming night:
in his mind's eye, irrigation channels sluice thin mirrors
round windy, green-headed paddocks. Drowsing,

he dreams that the air-hostesses bend over their rows
like a photo he once saw of 1940s cotton-pickers.
Each up-turned face is a nest of ugly beaks. Suddenly
waking, cloud wisps like drink trays float to his arm.

3. Lazarus

Put it down to a turn. The doctor showed me a map of stars,
asking if I could see their moving constellations, their pin-prick eyes,
the truth of their geometry across the woolshed on the station.
That's what it seemed like. If I could track them, I wasn't a mess.
So I traced them like doing an exam for school, to
show that I had learnt their names and that the edge
they moved across was still defined along a rifle's sight,
past the shed, on top of a ridge, down a fence. Things go wild
in the brain at points like these. The frame was fixed,
and that night sky kept growing and deepening like a floor
giving way beneath you. After the tests were over I got a taxi.

The next time and the next time, there was a queue.
I couldn't help but laugh. All these sick people, wanting an answer,
looking as if they were hugging something close to them: a ticket.
Or a reason to take the train into town and just wait a while.
More than the doctor, their fear gave me the frights –
that simple they'd stay for hours for the healer's touch,
a word of explanation, something prescribed, medical lingo.
Of course you want to know the science of death, but science
doesn't help when things go really crook: the doctoring profession
can only do so much with a neural system white-anted by disease,
or a mind already withdrawing from it, like a hawk soars.

I didn't go back. I'd got to that point. I thought I'd prefer
all the moments which, entombed, had stored what I would lose:
they'd said it would be gradual, an unnoticeable situation,
a farm shrinking after a set of bad years and growing expense.
I'd adjust to it over time and make the repairs I had to.
True, it's only a change of circumstances – a trip to somewhere
you've been when young – which gives you back nostalgic light.
There things stand out, naked and refreshed, and you feel

their presence at the very point it goes away: the shine on a bucket,
the distance you once walked, a sense of space. Sometimes I'd wonder
if I was already half-dead. And, then, if that thought too was pathology

making its way. So, you see, nothing had prepared me
for that day when, suddenly, as if being eaten alive by the air
or by the long blond skylines which closed up like a vacant limit
or by acres of saltbush whose tops, knee-high, extended like grey rubble
or by the sheen of dusty sunlight on miles of swaying grass
or by the phase of night and day splitting the pebbles at my feet
and exposing their nested, storm-dark eggs
or by the gulf of blue which each morning steadied its focus
before miraculously building fluffy clouds of swans on water,
I seemed to be walking youthfully again leading a thirsty horse,
a straggling flock, a dog circling like a fly. Out of the tomb.

4. Portrait of a True Republican

The second thing I remember is the sea,
very far away, across what might have been
a tidal marshland or Burrill Lake's estuary:
a wall of white light in the distance,
mirrored, flat water before it, mud-streaked sand.
It was nearly, or has become, pure sea dusk,
ocean low down, sparse as a shrub, catching
sun-glitter filtered backwards over dark hills,
I mean, how purple cabbage-clouds march landwards
leaving the water vacant as a fresh-wiped shelf.
Between clouds and sea the gap's as pale as sliced potato.
Again, like most early scenes, it's hard to distinguish
what's memory now from memory then: it's
one of those thought-about thoughts, much turned over
in half-conscious saying, in a life-long voice.
Someone perhaps told me about it, and I dreamt
this glimpse locked up, pastwards, like a photo.
Positioned, it fills in a childhood's story,
like weatherboard's cracked paint, a path's concrete –
a half-remembered novel read on a sunny back verandah –
all of them images of travel modes
still journeying with me years later:
now only the shining sea is fate's particular,
its snake-bright detail, lurking in knee-high grass.
I've no idea in fact why it's still there.

My earliest memory is being held up to see the Queen.
It was '53 or '54. Everyone was waiting on the platform.
I remember mostly chattery excitement,
blurred faces, a sense of clothes, a sense of where
that bit of paddock stood just opposite the half-built street.
Or maybe that was later – and it's got in there.
These days we'd do it for a stranded whale.

I remember the sudden lull, like quiet before a storm,
and that underwater-ish anthem of strained train tracks.
No doubt it all entranced a three-year old who'd
often been taken down to see the trains. Did anything happen?
I don't remember Mum and Dad's embarrassment.
They joked about it later when I was growing up:
it became the day we saw the Queen. We didn't.
A special train snaked through without slowing,
shipwrecking, blue as blood, the Hills' midday sky.

Whatever they are, memories make the light.
They're what we grow with. Imagine a life which can't change
given what you once had known of untouchable sea:
given the infrangibility of power.
This small thing is what you have, the future's
in half-conscious recollections of a room, a car,
a patch of sun upon a sleep-out's creaking planks.
Some hidden thoughts are illness you must live with,
others (like a freak wave) sweep you from the rock.
Another memory is of driving past a small sea-beach,
on a road straight as an arrow behind low dunes
in country of tall brown tussock, vermilion with late sun,
and the surf pouring its cream over glazed rocks.
For a while the skyline has a yellowish cinema glow.
Driving fast, a line of telephone poles flashes onwards.
The windscreen has nothing of childhood's sour demur.
A moment in a film, there is a sense of emptiness let in:
a nowhere contradicted by the rain's exposure
of a sandbank's midden, gleaming its oyster shells –
mosaic fragments, fishbone-white, sedimented.
One moment the whole thing stands in sudden depth,
as if, for a second, your eyes wander from the road,
the sun, the amber sea. Crazily, an emu appears
on the roadside by a spur. It seems to be waiting there
like a herald of the night. Next moment the sea, exploding,
bursts onto the land. A glance, quick as a wing, catches it.
Up front, darkness is voiced by a distant farm's first lights.

Rainbow Snake

for Peter Jacob

The blue vase keeps winking at me.
Varnished blueness does that to the eye.
Its blueness is a wilder sea, obscured
by curves and sheen. Blueness back of the surf,
with a gull hovering on water's moody heave.

Past sunset streaks, the vase gapes into air,
all ear to what might drown in it,
now turning sapphire in the shifting reds
which race across this gathering dark.
Now it gleams with lamp-light like a snake

camouflaged in the glitter of midday heat.
It takes the passing wings of flickering steps.
The vase stands there, shining, on the table.
Parts are like islands in a shadowy wash.
The body's razor-bright in changing dusk.

Sunset behind it deepens with a mallee glow.
Re-fired by skylines, it comes from the earth,
a bulb, taut, marked, sinuous. Each side's
again that snake. It bends time. Until about to soar,
pure thing, burnished as desert, it builds rock-towers.

Rice Fields Near Griffith

Mirrored clouds spike themselves with sharp, green shoots
in paddies marked out like holding tanks or Versailles' lakes.
Other fields nearby shine up broad, silver plaques.
Flooded, they're a smear over young plants. Bright as a knife blade,
glimmering like windows among unwatered, hazy country,
smooth as aluminium, these squares could be sheets of solar cells:
polythene, they could be sun-reflectors, hiding their works.
Getting out, stretching, I go for a leak and then a pointless walk.
I could be an accountant checking out holdings, properties, the eye's tracts,
but sight-seeing's really something no-one does round here. True,

all the way Major Mitchells sputtered their pinks along soft edges
while small towns' liquidambers dappled the car's interior.
Driving for hours in level country brings such change and rondure.
Found in dry parkland, an old tree with bark shaved for a canoe.
Over there, a blocked off swamp slowly kills a copse of semaphores.
The whole day, distance ("it's not far") has been like the ocean's curve
where someone's daylight-sailing without the help of stars:
for all that, plains make you feel true travel's underground.
What you see is Art Deco dream, investment, 1930s Federal plan,
parcels and sections, orange-farms' dark grooves, ruler-drawn frontiers

obvious from the air, and ever present right-angle boundaries
between flat green and flat dry: whichever direction you head
you'll reach that fence or irrigation ditch. What's steady is the road
cutting the horizon like a canal: no finger, it takes you dead straight
over this chequerboard, demanding its own *moderne*. Multiples
shrink to a glimpse, yet no Sydney high-rise has such scale.
At dusk there's the placement of Dutch-style, flowering polder-sunset,
with its furry smudge of bush-life – but drive like a truckie if you drive
        at night.
Even when you pull up you feel the place is still in motion,
a human map-space of layers, routes and risks where long journeys

bring quick returns. To think of parabolas is ridiculous.
(Besides, given the talk of water-tables, parables flow darker.)
Up top, wetlands for herons and ibis drown under abstract reservoirs,
while, beneath, hunting-grounds drift under drive-in vineyards.
Sugar-bag towns, long ago, gave way to mazes of leafy veneers:
a third generation already plans its museum. To get to the centre,
you must now unearth stories of hermits, Italian idylls, developers,
even if to someone, say, writing for *The Good Weekend* there's still the
        imagining
of a fertile world entirely portable, still affordable by artists,
drinking cool white de Bortoli, buying cases of wayside oranges.

Even a momentary glimpse reckons with drought hard as a scab.
Not tilth but tilt, seasons pass in cycles. Time's depth is palpable.
That's why, stopped by the music of these greens and sage-burnt dries,
in a vastness rich with crops of bird-calls and the spirit's circular towns,
with ground-pumps and the random drizzle of flies, my mind gets
focused on that grit-hard, unbleached seed in its husk
as if I'm suddenly trapped in the myth of the trekking explorer,
for whom every horizon was a meeting with despair's paradise,
bringing all too soon, after the period of the push west and squatters,
the ex-Indian parvenu-cum-relative and his engineer's tricks with water,

or as if recalling a few hours ago, I again pull up at the barrier of
a solitary river, hidden beneath the plain, marked by its ribbon of trees,
and having got out in the deserted picnic ground
there among the bow-lakes and muddy shadows of levees
I can't help but be fixed on details, on something incredibly small –
two water-boatmen jerking diagonally on the meniscus's brown glaze
a tossed Pepsi can bearing the weight of the hand which crushed it,
a hearth of rough stones from one of last summer's Rotary Bar-B-Q's –
till I lose touch with deceptive flatness, seeing only further out,
heat-bent trees float an inch over the grass-lands' bluest murky glass.

Forest Kingfisher

for Michael Cody

The fact that it made no noise
became what it said
including its moth-soft, blue cloak
flung up from a sawn stump,

just now perched there on an empty road,
hunched over with its back to us
as if staring at the sliver of orange-peel
poking across the ridge's see-through tree tops.

Its startled lift was as easy and sure as someone hoisting up
an empty cardboard box, surprised to find it light.
Unwitnessed silence was a falling amber leaf
there in that lonely turning of the road. Then, two things

occurred. First, it breathed itself into a bloodwood sapling
whose inner sprays were night enough to shelter it,
while outer leaves, quivering in late sun's butter-yellow storms,
marched pink surfaces against its splay of azure wings.

Caught, it lodged itself under a wedge of sideways glare,
where aqueous light had pierced the dusty turpentines.
Next, fearing we'd found it, it launched across the space
like someone flying a kite against shattered sun and wind:

it shot itself out of that sapling's nowhere camouflage
escaping from last light's shell-burst like a fighter pilot,
a blue javelin freezing the clearing's glassier patches,
heading onwards to where unnoticed flood swamps glimmered

like coins beneath the trees. It swerved diagonally
across those wells. It was an eye, a glance. It
unleashed its way of being-now; its ghostlike richness,
its stillness flying behind all language that's trained or pure:

blue-jacketed kingfisher, it made off like a scratch on a lens
into an uncovering between eye and mind – *bugeen, muleemah* –
as if it had found a hidden, remembered pathway
down a river bend's once clear light and the trees' sunset fire.

Australia

for Robert Gray

Beneath the wings dust storms pile up Spanish walls
in long, angry scuffs of brushed brown paint
bristling two hundred miles south to Alice.
Next, non-stop sunset unmoors its cloud-falls
into floating alligator jaws till, northwards, dark land's
pitted with diamonds, pinpoints of lights, and pearls.

The plane's as slow and drowsy as a fly on a table,
and, there beneath, the desert looks like a sea's ebbed out,
undoing all classic truths from this strange angle
in the odd perspective of 20th Century travel –
nothing at all like lorikeets and screeching parrots
when they search, with green streaks, air's pale exit.

For a few moments, there's flat darkness plus a kind of depth
where things are marks like road lines between two bores,
mountains are upturned mushrooms, white with sun.
Soon, uncleared coast is spanned by a moon-walker's step,
while sea's an Eskimo's fishing hole cut in an ice-field,
glimmering upwards its wrinkled mother-of-pearl

into which river-mouths wind miniature ribbons of silt,
fanning out in a duck's-foot webbing. In fact,
it's hard to know if that coastal darkness is trees or shadow,
harder still to know if the sense of being slow and separate
comes from flying out or from dusk's melancholy.
I always have this feeling when I'm on the plane.

It seems incredible. A realist won't have it this way:
the saucer you look at is bizarre immensity,
shrunk down to a dot or a dusk-coloured patch.
Later, when night comes on it trails you like a stray,
or as if it's trapped you in its permanent pre-dark phase.
It's like a rip you can't get out of close to shore.

This could, of course, be tiredness not just the flight,
together with vague ideas of an unplanned future –
kitsch destiny which such a home-made trip brings on.
Rather, it's finality. It's the sense you must get right
all those judgements you have made for years, like
some half-paid art critic doing his rounds. I do it all the time.

Sure, in the '60s, the Antipodeans leapt on the sky,
skimming the mallee, or helicoptering the North-West.
They brought back huge canvases of carmine glare
with plains of knotted threads, creeks like thighs,
where there was no border to a mythic prospect
of frontier wheat-lands, mule-dead creeks, desert saltpans:

they found at least something large enough to see
in a horizon which drowns Uluru's rain-red pebble,
painting light as if it's a medium you look down through
till a vast thing swims in the smallest eye.
There the eye travels like a tractor crawling down below
and a hawk studies it, hovering, unwilling to fall.

Flying, I have this image now of dry, transversal plains.
Edgeless night comes on and travels with the jet.
At the back of my mind, the shock of river water
or, whiter than gull shit, last year's flood stains
draining towards Lake Eyre: it's the clutter
of half-thoughts I bring with me. Re-made satellite shots.

Down there iconic lands erased by sheep flocks grazing
into west wind, leaving a mark as big as Sicily.
Street sounds move in my sleep like a curtain.
Even my backyard's pool cakes on a filmic haze.
If asked to summarise, I'd speak of new world futures,
gay lifestyle, Desert painting, Federal land rights.

Call it perhaps, then, a well-off, livable Argentina
with its shards of myth set up in export mode
to old oceanic powers and new high-rise neighbours,
a dry fringe whose dimensions upset the television,
whose multitudinous doubt's as learned as traditional art,
and where we can't afford 68ers, or the classicist's smirk.

It's easy to parody. Our desert winds bloom camp cinema.
Sumatra's sunset flash dazzles sharp, remembered skylines.
Yet, in shifts of line and sound, I find that landspeak
on the route of an aerial, half-invented Dreaming
which names our taste for light: a dry-country love,
where fences run to the horizon, lightly, beyond the West.

A Studio in Prague

for Mirek Jiranek

Plaited bread where
braided strands of dough fold over each other –
toasted, yeasted, aerated with heat –
often woven wreathlike in the form of an eternity-circle
or corded into the shape of a Corn God
or a Celtic Cross (in rural areas
of those countries famous for vampires it's an art
practised for centuries though not yet subsidised); or

the vertigo
of imagining each intersected angle
of body and movement in galaxies
speeding away from each other like bubbles in a cascade of water
pouring through light and time, on an axis
neither up nor down nor flat, so you must –
if you'd grasp night's sheltering raft of darkness –
also invent scarves of energy flung in space; and the

rabbit-warren
of wires, plugs, circuits, dots, thresholds, systems,
matrices, formats, nets, addresses, boxes,
states, cells, storages, memories, most of them burning away
and open to the air, supporting surfaces
glinting like the wastes you drive over in Poland
when its lakes, snow-fringed with wedding-cake ice,
echo with sunset-wind soughing in birch trees; – can all of them

be reduced to
a glass of milk spilt on a polished table
when you reached over for a crayon? It was a flash-moment,
a flesh-moment. A moment of Zen inspiration. Well it became
this little disaster. But the trams kept on running in the street,
wilful snow flakes kept hovering outside the window –
down below, people queuing at the stops. All your thought
was of making your picture as soon as possible

while messages
ran east and west, while stars made their nests
over the Steppes' farms, while malleable dough rose and roasted
in its oven. Under your hand, each grass-blade stood out, diamond-like,
on a slope where warm wind reared and tossed –
bob-tailed rabbits could dig there, Mongolian horses graze –
though there wasn't a path anywhere in its huge, green shield.
A green slope stood there, wholly visible. It was a mind's forest, the eye's:

now back in Sydney,
nudged by winter blue in a half-baked video,
I remember most your painting's skyline while having a fit of the dumps
about how automation is loss of power when set against
the yearlong limning of expression, voice, hope,
practised in your more ancient style of studio
after wasting a day (you know, an American-style workshop)
watching TV philosophers at work on their highway.

Leeches

They like damp grass, overhanging trees,
boggy pathways, areas without run-off
they camouflage themselves in twigs, leaves, dirt.
They hang like rubber-bands from bushes,
they sniff you by the edge of the creek.
God's creatures, they're bloodsuckers.
In your shoes they swell like maggots:

fat, soft, stubby. You can't snap them.
Pull them and (as in snake nightmares)
they change shape, they become more,
they become longer. Pliant to be firm,
they're pastry strings, overcooked pasta:
ideal matter, they're basic in design –
projects for multiples, for being sure,

for randomness. They're very '90s.
Independent, survivors of drought,
they multiply in flood conditions:
they live quietly till they whiff flesh.
Then their tubes erect and their mouths
suck, adhere to, kiss, bruise
any skin which seeps blood. From

being arch-backed, negative, expectant,
they become a swarm. You brush one off
to find another. They pop out like stars.
If they could, they'd be permanent,
returning like shape-changing morphs
whose concept is rain-shower or swamp.
Their bite is velcro. I'm sure, in fact, they're

universal force. If old Galen knew
them as health kicks – as we use fibre diet –
it's likely their role as steady clients
(they search for any source passing by)
makes them vital models for transport,
dispersal, cell-growth. When I discover
them on me, I go round the bend:

out in wet bush, they can be everywhere
yet hidden at the same time. Art,
too, exploits a certain rich dividend:
invention's about naming the air,
the vacuum, with realities, yet
to be identified. Text-book leeches. Right now, though,
I still see them as false, climbing friends.

View from Point Piper

Apart from the workings of old moods,
the fruit bowl placed by the window,
the ants, like filings, on white formica
in the yellow gauze of March's slanting warmth,

smallness, infinitesimal smallness, is
the arc of daily living, daily life.
Coffee, work, views, change of light.
Today a call from down the coast.

Back of them, a scene I mostly ignore,
too familiar with its moods, its yachts,
knowing some things must be left
to flower and fruit in silent heat:

a harbour mirroring spandrels of light
from three clouds back of the point.
Beneath surfaces, the blackest space.
Within desire, a wind like fire in grass.

Daily life. Daily moods. Blink and
the whole world blinks with you.
Amber sunset over waves of rippling wheat,
the horizon, hawk-like, settles in one place.

Images

1. TV At Night

"When someone's lost at sea the heartache's endless,"
warbles the mother from Alabama in a close-up. Next, the announcer
says the yacht was sighted long after the coast-guard called an end.

Everyone hopes the drowned one will be found
in a spume of white flowers, in a new news flash on TV.
A brown spinnaker drips. Pure heartache's announced,

"My daughter was lost at sea." Everyone hopes that the drowned girl lives,
that it's just an accident and that accidents
are snow-storm interference, and the causes quickly found:

somehow the cyclone didn't lash the front, the endless
palm-trees resumed their upright, the surf started breathing down the beach.
Fresh-faced, the young blond will walk out of the surf in her pink
            Bermudas, announcing

not that she's become an eternal repetition of the end,
but that she's still a figure whose love was never accident.
Unconched Aphrodite, she gracefully steps along the sand. A loop. A love.

Waiting to greet her, there's Hawaii 5-0's instant black-tie beach party where
daiquiris are constantly announced. Then there's a break. No more
            accidents are found.
(Flashed between ads, this repeat episode's a look-alike, an ending without end.)
Horse-mane waves bristle forward, purple, with phosphor, glittering.

Soon of course the twist – smugglers, drug-trafficking – is threaded in.
Rotten as the jaws of tropic sea, a rusty Panamanian-licensed steamer
floats past Tahiti. Hastily painted, the boat's name keeps changing

in the way that vowels warble, or in the way that Alabama mocking-birds
and English nightingales
chant their themes in poems of the night, distilling their descants,
extending their accents backwards even into the bayou's steamy waters,
tinting all old photographs, all old ports, all old news. They, too, urge
        their end:

She's dead, she's dead, she's dead, they sing, pulsing their notes from spinning
        shells
of satellites, from light through tape. Their songs can be found
in any forest. It's not just TV upsets me. It's that mother's hag-like voice
        once more announcing

the word against which survivors hope that screens, at least, don't end,
screens being endless as the clash and leakage of images are endless,
endless as fish swimming in shoals over red, swaying tentacles,

endless, too, as this vast continent's water-table which raises and lowers
        itself through its compacted layers,
immeasurable as distance between a transmitter and a car-yard of sceneries,
uncountable as the corrugations of sheet iron roofs in, say, an Indonesian city,

recurrent as night's mile-long waves, up here, at surf-striped Hawks Nest,
where outside, in fringes of the National Park, banksias bear hard, fish-
        mouthed fruit
while, indoors, insomniac night wind still chatters on never about-to-
        close TV.

2. Red Roses

Though I've lived in many places, there are no epitaphs.
Instead of the poem of exile and renewal,
there is this: how today, before waking, I dreamt again of fires

burning high-country corn fields. In all directions, smoke-plumes
rain-spouted the horizon. It struck me
as a TV image of desert mountain war – a simple thing,

a fragment which couldn't be gainsaid, a flower, a hybrid.
Half-grasped, this image came from ruins of the past.
In my flat, all through the Bosnian war, I saw it night by night –

that time, in files of women, men, children from the destroyed areas
lumbering forward on horse-drawn carts with rubber wheels.
Or in snow-humped graves strewn with flickering, red roses.

As through fretwork in an ancient window,
light fell on me from what I saw. (Not Sydney's angophora- and sail-on-
        water light.)
Not one, but a grille of images flashed their colours,

setting each other off, exploding, blowing the body apart.
And it was the dream-cortex, only, which masked
those slaughterous zones of power – these were only the atrocities

of things seen. A kaleidoscope, perhaps. Or someone else's memories
Like personal history, it seemed that finally they'd acquired a half-lived form:
war, murder, nation, crime. In the dream, smoke, flame, blood, TV sceneries

became a splinter in the mind – a fantasy-bit
left over when the day was done:
a film-strip of Kabuls, Cambodias, Rwandas, Iran-Iraqs, Kuwaits.

They were the zones in which my hybrid image grew.
Product of the mode of endless vision, others call it latency,
in which the truth is dark, blind, or displaced unspeakably –

until, that is, I woke. This dream is mine
or anyone's. A half-thought troubling me,
it's like a vector passing through space, cleaving its line.

What's left is a memory of roses, red, red roses.
This is the image which stays –
unwrapped flowers strewn on the earth, offering the presence

of the angel's folded wings and the dead eye's gaze
at *hic iacet's* and *Thus I suffered's*. Thus, round the world, a decade's psyche
builds up its reef of coral flowers. And always

so many monsters, rising from the deep,
growling into that dawn-lit zone
between the latest facts and turning back to sleep:

dear citizen, I was nor heartless or indifferent. This, a message from now.

The Platypus

The gift of tongues and sight is platypus.
The gift's unusual, including mountainous
flowering wattle under feral elm trees,
amber water varnishing emu-egg stones,
dawn's acanthus-leaf cloud after tramping miles
to spy on rare animals, once unprotected:

flat-footed platypus, *Gr.* for "walking problem,"
botanist Banks gave it to Napoleon.
Its history's famous. Paradox or thorn
in the side of Victorian scientists,
now it's a cute, duck-billed rarity,
an icon for postage stamps. Imagine it, then,

an animal too finely balanced to be seen.
If you want a lithe, underwater Kieran
Perkins – it's a platypus. If you're keen
on Chinese acrobats, you've yet to see
a platypus chasing droplets like a kitten
playing mock kills with a tangled ball of wool.

Platypus also carries with it streaks
of dawn's cinder-glow on water, ferrying creaks
with its alligator-style head. It's no snake's.
Sultry daybreak, dusk's pink slants, are the times
for its water-beetle chase, at one with noiseless
swallows darting over the stream's bakelite shadow.

Unlike them, it can shift from one medium
to another – from scrabble to dig to swim.
Fur, blood, bones, it lives out a warm theorem:
how cells communicate with mode and shape.
It's pure exuberance of style. No post-modern,
it benefits from natural history. No victim,

it even shows how to adjust thoughts to
that *maya,* that dream, where illusion's both true
and false: too much attachment and you
are gnawed by anger, striving with an aqueous
world which shape-shifts like a plant stem, angled
in a glass tank. Too little attachment and

the transparent creek shines up front, soundless
as the visual nightmare of images
which form TV-adapted, bionic eyes.
A moon-traveller's eyes. This, too, is platypus,
scumbling up through a fire-flecked, weedy drift,
paddling, swerving like a diver, to the air.

Then, back down. Better than the funerary
swimmer at Paestum, it slides under memory:
it can regain depth. Lost from sight, it must be
tracked with a torch light under mirrored ledges,
where white roots dangle, raw as bull-dozed forest –
there it penetrates its world of water-sky –

darting through silhouettes of wobbling banksias and heath,
swimming on a knife-edge of height and width.
It's pelt-shadow. Air bubbles track its breath.
Ducks have bills, female spiders poison, but the
platypus combines worlds in its metaphor
of doing several things well. So you tramp miles

in the hope of seeing it: wilderness's smoky blues
give it its moment. It's placed as platypus.
In the National Estate it swims and burrows,
dark bat spread-eagled beneath light's dream surface,
as it rummages through its household water,
urged on, back of the mind, at home. Pure, dumb sex.

Yachts at Scotland Island

for Marcia Stewart

After a day of Greek references, lunch, and Freudian puns
the *mythoi* aren't appropriate to the dapple and sting-rays
any more than to a brain verbalising everlastingly
on its right-side stones and its left-side waters. But, no less,

the TV, modernity's end, the abolition of craft in networks –
all those roadways through intelligent starlit places –
are short meeting-spaces with cartoon characters
hanging in trees, or just the other side of the bay.

I read *Soundsite, Leonardo, Fanzine* and *MLA.*
Outside, water noise ripples in flickering rosemary bushes.
Inside, the modem chatters in its own drifting sky.
Sometimes it's a frog by a creek. My hand glides with its mouse.

Smart theorists, like hang-gliders, call this sensory geography
which maps travel through the texts which build it, a place
of fire in which the passageways are infinite yet framed.
There's no closeness. Or too much. A pack of cards, a street vanishes.

Appliances are light and portable. You need nothing.
Not just the heat, you dress in sleeveless shirts and go barefoot.
Even to work is to study fragments which are locked, submarine,
while the air's cinematic forest jangles its symbols of light –

tempting, though, to invent new worlds through patched-up bits,
floating in a medium less real than water. Names are tags,
which once were metaphors, for views down the road,
for the boss, for the book or the sea: or rather, for rags

weightlessly falling as in the last scene in that Antonioni movie,
where the whole house explodes like a flight of birds.
What's left is its owner's first risky choice, a Mojave Desert view.
It was the desert there which gave the sense of distant clouds.

Myself, too, I usually work my best far away from water.
I prefer it as one element among dry-country scapes
which here only the pathway's European rosemary reminds me of –
like a mallee sunset over a plain of yellow-flowering rape

whose sharp, flat skyline becomes a shimmering lake and burns,
or, air-borne, like the sense that an ancient tide's exposed the Olgas,
sculpted by sand storms and the air's weight. Residues which repeat,
even this use of drifting, underwater images is a sign of our times:

that is, until a slow-building change occurs towards mid-afternoon,
shifting the glare in the grey gum overhanging the verandah
and spilling out pale blue hammerheads over blunt, green slopes.
Perhaps I get up to close the windows. Somewhere, a minah-

bird starts to fret. There's a tropical stillness. Then branches move.
Briny, the heat comes on moody, heavy, grey as a porpoise,
inclining the yachts in leeward wind as if they're random shapes,
abstract triangles like styrofoam chips, fleeting, behind glass:

you see them caught in a bar of choppy wavelets – it's like a wedge –
or frozen on a water-shelf, dark as the Sargasso's and as strange.
Now, as the wind whips up, they make their way to the channel,
where the ocean they engrave slops about in a white meringue.

It was Plato (that dramatist) who first distinguished place from space,
granting the latter its deathly power of giving, mapping, taking away,
imagining it as a sieve sifting the threshed Just-Nows –
a wall of brightness landing across stormy, green-chipped wakes,

or a fruitful, black bulb of laden sea-cloud about to burst its charge.
The yachts sail away under it like ducks gliding on a shooting-range.
Conscious of the change, I shift the pointers on the flowing screen
and log instructions for a letter which needs ten seconds to Brisbane,

half-catching only the suspense of the quick, unnoticed tuning
by which the wind's simplest shiver across the grey gum is a voice,
still whispering as it once did: Yes, I wait at the known world's pillars.
Or: A boat of flowers bearing you, I am the old man's winnow.

Stopping for a Walk in
Reserved Land Near Murra Murra

It's a stop-over on a Spring day
when, walking through the bush, I see them.
Bees. Wild bees, already clustered,

already swarmed. A galaxy of living honey,
they hang on a branch
in a swollen, brown gourd, a primitive shape

caught on the move. All gouache, clay, and bubble,
it's hard to fix it for what it is,
frightening to imagine stumbling into its pelting dust

just landed out of the horizon's blue nowhere,
now settling above dwarf ti-tree, above red earth.
Pummelled soil, hanging between sky and ground,

it takes on a flickering, gold-dyed sheen,
gold as if a shock of tinted hair's
been threaded, quartz-like, through its ochre mass: bodies, heads, legs,

writhing on each other, pinioned there.
It's as if each body mimics a future cell.
Or as if the air has opened up a hasty, war-time grave

where corpses, tossed into the pit, drown each other
with their awkward, rotting limbs.
This swarm is that exposed. That stark.

A wattle-and-daub affair, compacted
in a furious swerve
to a taller tree's white branch, the swarm hangs there

sandstorm-brown,
a haze of movement
and molecules. It's as sharp and deafening

as if all the body's sensations arrive
at one go, or as if a life-time's
thoughts are suddenly, spontaneously, recalled

by someone moving, at the very edge of life,
when the mind's
sky-white with memories, swelling with

the fruit of experience, swarming
at death,
yet holding all feelings together;

or as if, veil-like, it's summed up later (generations later,
after the earth
has soaked up spilt blood and honey streams)

by the philosopher who says:
Things are not things,
but groups, sets, swarms, flux –

playing their music of ant
and bird. The swarm
is light. It's energy, fruit of the desert's edge.

Fruit, indeed, is fruit. And whether
in grief or orgy,
these bodies pile on top of each other:

they're a huge brown pear,
they're an outsize bobbin of unwashed flax,
hanging from a yellow-gum.

It takes for ever to focus on. It swirls.
It implodes in the branches,
hanging there like a wind-harp

of silk-glitters and half-dried mud
with outriders taking off and returning,
like flies to a carcase. Not beautiful,

dark, full of anger, full of sting.
it changes shape
like a pot spun between invisible hands,

slowly growing bulbous, then tapering to a narrow neck,
in danger of falling apart
or attacking like a Mongol horde

yet still clustering, still forming itself
from Spring's exile
and the struggle of poisoned virgin grubs –

till it steadies its larval magic
into an Earth-Mother drone
of particles, dynamos, ancestral flight.

A Month in the Country

Sharp squawks of two rosellas come in with me.
Away from the heat, the outside looks pale and aqueous.
Inside the house, spaces are functional, lived-in:
split-level living, white formica of a dream kitchen,
rimmed round by a verandah giving three feet of shade.
Beyond it, a line of whitewashed, battering light
becomes a ladder of ripples up the water tank.
The sink's a glittering plain even the ants avoid.
Waiting to grow, the protection for this side
is a flag-stand of sapling gum trees, still as a crate.

It started differently. Dawnlight: a flamingo slab
where Assyrian glyphs floated on tree-silhouettes –
a sense of see-through puppet-show, with clouds on sticks.
Turning over, I woke to caterpillar tracks,
far flung in coolness, stalking intemperate blue.
Now, away from the outside's drench of light and noise,
the house's anchored stillness is like a river boat's
till the fridge rattles, switching off its cool and heat,
unbalanced, needing to be fixed. It's a tad too warm
to think of it today. All day, this heat was coming.

An off-the-shelf design, the house rides out my mood:
I'm caretaking for friends, gone overseas.
Their orchard's already planted near a dried up gully –
there's a conservationist half-flush in each loo –
and everywhere signs that they're planning long years
of toddlers' bikes parked on the back door's patio.
These are professional dreams of a two-pump town:
Pajero-land with phone, the main taps town-supplied.
But inside, there are smooth plains of polished wood
a homeliness where the everyday looks tranquil,

uniform, used – the kitsch sliding screen doors,
doubling for Christmas beetles and security,
or the wood-stove harking back to up-country times,
when fire wood wasn't ever green. Hard to make,
easy to undervalue, it's a new Colonial,
built from near-perfect, unreturning richness.
Half-Bush, half-City, it floats between passion and loss.
No, it'll never deliver the Country Dream.
Yes, true love's debris clutters the ear-marked family room.
There are fresh scars of bull-dozed earth. A pool half-built.

So I go inside. Finding their tree, rosellas shriek
like a detail or a thought I can't get back to:
a hairline crack, an edge of trees, a cloud-wisp's smudge.
Heavy brilliance, overhead, perfects its image
in a few seconds of stillness. Out of nowhere,
a late change might happen, building its haze.
It's not so strange, then, that what catches up with me
is also out of the blue, an electric atmosphere
which builds and builds, unseen like the click of a shutter,
or a blurred thought, steadily brought into mind –

how I've been travelling away from my mother,
highways melting to the smoothness of water,
daybreaks white as saltpans, white as air,
features which, as you drive there, only disappear.
Her death, years gone, is like an outcrop speeding away.
It's seen so differently each time I look.
Long past grief, I hold to grief's inner history,
sudden pain blossoming from something already finished –
a flower-strewn corpse, a memory calcified.
That's what it is. A grief-sense, beneath things, flashes back

in a memory of years of illness, themselves like death,
with all my senses frozen, mirror-like, in glass.
I've watched others build anew after the process,
out of families (like my own) classic as *Sons and Lovers*.
Trauma squeezes the heart tight. Time's blank sky
tears down the walls. Nothing is left after the fire.
Like bone cancer, grief fills the brain with razor-light.
It wipes out each start-up frill of cloud-shaped loaves,
each blue-green wing-flutter, each thought of uncupped leaves,
till caught in dying light, maternal, all fear stops.

The Red Gum

A camera could catch it. Or a video. A painter can't.
It's October's first dry wind, blowing in across the Harbour.
Rousing, irritable wind, with the feel of flat country out west,
it thrashes the red gum with its tentacle flowers, its blood-red new leaves,
whose images will never be finished, never held, even
by the best of visualists. The reds of this red tree
dazzle and blur, both cochineal and stain of flying-ants.

I'm stuck with this red tree. These blue waters. Everything's primary.
Gusts and gusts of invisible wind shake the branches
into horse-heads neighing and rearing into shoals of silver –
let loose, they're mares floury with dusty evening light
under trees, in a paddock, back of the mind. Spring wind blasts them,
turns them back to main-street bunting rattling, triangular, overhead.
It crackles the leaves like a fire that's burning up too fast, too dry.
Against grey-blue water, the red gums sinewy branches shine.
Behind it, yacht masts and yellow water taxis cutting their wakes.
Across the bay, particles of cars glide by, silent as a museum's dust.

I make coffee, think of the washing. I'll spend the day looking at pictures:
slides of someone's work. There'll be lunch, maybe an hour at the pool.
All the while, the red tree flickers and threshes, an image from a shaky aerial.
Against the blue, its curtain's like a crimson smear, a fishing-net of shadows.
All morning the flat is full of slanting diamond light and sun,
probing, like a philosopher, this side and that. A wall, a bit
of floor, a bookshelf: and, then, again the tree,
like a gigantic window-cleaner, looming at the window. No Oak
of Dodona, its variable upsets pure prophecy. Its clouds glitter,
promising richness, quite other than a tranquil view
taken in across the land: a prospect of water-meadows,
a few cows. Or a portrait with brilliant drapery. Who was it
said the wind is "boneless?" This ghost's rattling its maraca,
making words impossible. For all the time, this storm-tossed red gum
burns its way into the mind, under thought and reference,

like a premonition you can't tease out:
its own forest of sun-lit fire, taking over everything around it,
whether neighbouring roofs, or the gulls battling to the Heads,
with rain-storms of flowers hanging out, drily, for heat and bees.
Just for a second, it's static under cloudless light, golden as a haystack.

Remembering Floodwater

Back of the mind, it's the white sliver which is
neither misty trace nor meaningless: it probably
isn't snow, nor that glare effect of a white line
which the sea's horizon can sometimes have
on days when the air's clear as untouched cellophane.
It's a particular white sliver, or smear of white,
like a patch of sand bunting through leaf-cover,
held forever, remembered, from some walk years back.
It's the stripe of light on sandhills towards dusk,
caught just once, recalled, seen again somewhere else.
Or it's untouchable shadow on the white metal of the roof
of the house next door, a shadow that's also a silhouette
of a bougainvillea, cascading red flowers
down the walls, overgrown round the drain pipes –
and, above the roof, three pelicans hanging in the sky
as if they're boats moored in wind-slopped water.
This is the brightness I usually wake up to, or
which wakes me, after a night of dreamless sleep.
I slept like that last night. After weeks away,
I wake up once again in a house tranquil as summer,
a house full of things (lamps, sinks, chain, doors)
which do not need to sleep. Just for those first
few moments, after I've come into the kitchen,
everything's as calm and cool as the fridge.
Then it hums, quietly, and the lazy, gliding pelicans
flap their wings. It could be once or for ever,
like a particular sensation which arrives and goes,
before it's anchored, then felt again. Getting back,
I've that feeling that somehow things
have changed when really they haven't:
perhaps they should have changed. They haven't.
You're still asleep. The neighbour's roof offers
back a little ultraviolet to the unsmudged blue,
while I'm thinking of the time away, the journeys,

the days and days on arid, high-speed roads. It could be
you're dreaming of it right this moment, curled over
like a slope of land. Nothing changes. Or perhaps it's country light
that's burned itself behind my eyes. Now the trace
becomes that sliver. Like a shadow getting through
the lids, I remember spilt-out glaze on flooded wetlands
with their dead, grey trees still standing there
and ibis cruising down to land. A string of fence posts
wades into the water's middle, before it drowns. Up close,
two swallows, scissoring, vanish across the sun.

Travelling Out West

Driving up to Griffith, the problem isn't vision
even if cars up front hang at midday on a moonlit-coloured road.
Oncoming, they're smears behind watery headlights,
in full approach capturing a sultry mood.

Out here, rare moments must duplicate for things.
Even the smallest object becomes personal memory,
and you start searching for details not loaded with time,
for moments of parrot-flicker, or for the mind's agility

in coping with distance made of stops and starts. Instead,
there's a sense of hours consumed, of isolated features:
tiny changes in the tree-line chatter away to you.
while the country's fringed, flat saucer is the greatest barrier

broken only by a farmhouse's tidy paint, a road's placement,
by a main street's Sunday-like vacancy or unused sidings.
There's always a whole day in which to get there
over xylophones of wooden bridges, loose planks rattling.

After hours of it, though, you start to be technical
about water-levels, yellow rosellas, river red-gums;
about rice paddies, infested, smooth as green silk;
about orange orchards' regiments; mostly, about floating visions.

visions which shimmer, brimming with bulging light,
aluminium sharp as a glasshouse, shiny as a new tractor.
If there's mystery, it's buried in the land's experiment.
When sunset happens, it's like film, burning, jammed in a projector,

but then it turns into sheets of redness stretched across the air.
Amber sun's shrunk to an eye, the Cyclops' eye of a diesel.
Bells rung at a crossing. Like eye-dazzle, swallows flicker.
Stagnant as canals, sideroads are straight as a gun-barrel.

Totally operatic, waterpumps fling up white arms
of water in the background of gauzed vineyards:
small-town life proffers the motorist an Art Deco cinema,
a fenced-in cemetery's solitaire, plantations of cheap wood,

and a horizon over a road going one direction,
using up time as if measured only in momentum.
Such travelling magnifies energy which flashes like a slide.
Perhaps in a poem you'd rather study a classic urn.

But if so, you miss how waterholes capture a tinted monocle,
how air-bombed clouds of fertiliser burst like wind-bristled snow,
how sea-dusks are sea-dusks flowing far inland,
how the built thing, the crafted vase, blinds the eye's fixity.

Night's Paddock

When we meet at night,
this is what I feel:
you are moving under dark trees.
I am those trees, those shapes.
You're the stars moving down the plain.

You're the stars moving behind
the motion of that move,
the inwardness of mood
by which stars and night modify
their space inside a moving mark,

a restless mark, a figure of moons,
of present and absent moons,
of darkness shining on the water tank,
of dark motion at the edge
of dark matter, holding it, cupping it

as if it's water-glitter in the mind
or a single thread of memory
moving like a herd across the dust:
my own night within me,
miles of fences under the night hovering.

Moon Gazing
in Sorrento Dusk

Moon Gazing in Sorrento Dusk

i.m. Roland Robinson

The first moon was what it had always been: a trick.
No shield of stars or snakes wrapped round each other,
a skein-moon floated in a dotted warmth of black.
Light-stealer, it wasn't an authentic. Floating
above the clumped-up she-oak shapes, it shone
in white space above the swan's-wing cloud,
an illustration of how much light it takes
to cast dark shadows on an empty, boat-strewn beach.
Yes, cliché-moon, it shines across Port Phillip's green water,
competing with the distant promontory of streets.
Fuller now, it wedges its amber path across the bay,
blending pale turquoises with currents smooth as glass.
Less a stairway than a glittering spill of pipe clay stripes,
it turns the surface into a map of body-shapes.
Only the wooden jetty casts its warning finger
out across that sloppy mix of stipple-marks and fire.
Bluish air tints the boat-house at its end.
The moonlight slips beneath it, glares it out,
making it a shadow of struts and weed-clung slats
over huddled gleams and sheep-back waves.
The moon, though, keeps on coming up, keeps on soaring,
quietening the memory of sunset's wattle birds,
dulling the woodsmoke smell of winter mist.
Now it's a disc flying the once red-gated west
scattering the arid centre's richness, pouring its floods,
over the harbour-zone, climbing a mud-soft cliff.
Heading from rock-plug country, it deluges its animal-crowds.
It is a whiteness smeared on the suburb's scar-burnt flesh.
Next, it ripples over the ground building it up again and again,
making it hard to walk over even the slants of a twig,
exposing a micro-world of fallen things and flakes.
Snail-moon, it sings itself into the night, casting its sliding track.

•

The other moon was a goanna-shape. I saw it years ago,
late one night by a campfire down Kangaroo Valley.
It came up over the river, flickering, spreading its quiet.
This moon had the crackle of unfathomed summer dark,
casting black-white geometries on turpentines:
its milky flowers were pathways over slopes,
opening new ledges of light and shade, building them
from saw-tooth shadows thrown by bottlebrushes.
This full moon brought with it stillness soft as a glove,
finer than any wind could breathe through empty dark.
Here each falling leaf pattered its wirebrush tympany.
The rustle of a paddy melon was picked up yards off.
Touchable dark, it was a night of careful movement,
a night with no fear of human shadow. Its stillness
was moon-faced owls. It was a bush-rat night.
My fire burnt its logs to rib-cages and ashen swamps,
sputtering quick fireflies towards a canopy of veins –
snapping gunshots out across the gully
where two possums quarrelled, jumping tree to tree.
All round me, too, crickets clinking, whispering,
over inaudible water sliding by through darkness,
It was only the moon-flow, poured through branches,
which brought to mind how such a movement's also noise,
its alkaline light setting limits to what you'd see,
mapping the forest not by bulk but by outline,
mapping the floor with bends and ponds of light,
disconnected like a half-dried-out river of terraced pools.

This moon – moon-white, camouflaged goanna – dobbed itself in,
there on a nearby tree-trunk, plastered to its bark,
embracing it like a toddler clinging to his father's leg.
melting itself into strips of light, into silhouetted wood,
upright, vertically pinned, along the cool, tall trunk.
It had got there without me seeing it, planting its shield
on a surface which, like webbing, could give it shelter,
hiding its four-foot-long tail, striped like a hand club,
painting itself on cleft and ridge, on funnelled grooves,

as if the growing fibre was earth beneath its claws,
as if its breathing flanks were leaf shapes flickering,
with all its muscled wrestler's strength flattened down
into a single pattern hanging on that dappled wall,
making its leathery snout press against the sap
so tightly that it played quite dead though I moved up close,
watching me in its smug, split way through starless eyes
until at last it slithered further, clutching at the bark's crumbling scabs
moving to lurk on the tree's moonless side. Then,
quick as a whip, powered by thighs and upper-tail,
it shifted in a mountain-climber's scramble to a fork
between two boughs where the light was smooth and hollow:
a fat body-builder, thug clambering away out of the torch light,
reptile marked with home-made designs, tattooist in solitary,
night-time dancer painted in his warrior's finery,
prisoner of light. Perched up there, it was a flake of moon.

•

Hiding up a tree, some moons kill their wives' children,
drowning them in a black lake's fishing-net of shadows.
Often this moon goes on his name-giving package tour
with someone who's a true companion – an interstate backpacker –
up till the final quarrel which separates two travellers,
mortal from ancestor, subject from thing, flesh from milky idea:
but, really, we know the moon's a young girl, one of two,
escaping into the bush from a half-mad, sex-starved rapist.
She's gathering bulbs when Rainbow Carpetsnake grabs her.
Then she's placed in the moon, pregnant, perhaps rewarded
for wrong-doing carried out by ancestor figures on death's river.

This moon's also late afternoon's thumb-print moon, tissue-thin,
a painter's accidental smudge up there across the Pacific,
hanging out for his star-friends, hanging out for his fire-glitter
to break across lacework-and-mother-of-pearl surfbacks.
Before you know, it's spinning into a night of darker floods.
It changes appearances, shadows, surfaces, its own height.

One such, it splashed across the sky at Avoca, two years ago,
turning the wires of a nearby fence into mobile strings,
making even a spider's web a phosphorescent target,
putting into each wave-flow a tiny inverted yacht-sail:
it was a breakthrough moon, November's, sharper than headlights,
one of those now-you-see-me-now-you-don't moons
which had followed me up the coast, hiding inside she-oaks,
or dodging under a dog-black ridge the other side of inland water.
It watched from hideouts along the freeway's smooth skin.
Moon-like as a recurrent thought, it rose from memory: it
was the moon of eternal knowledge. It was fixed, clear.
Everything about it was the opposite of how I felt.
I felt only how the blood dries and nerves collapse,
taking body-movement, breath, lungs, feeling, with them,
how the eyes dying close to a lizard's thin slits,
how, already worn, the world's an old stone step,
and how all light's a daybreak light of water-thin colours.
It was one of those moments which happen to any of us,
bringing a sudden sense of fragility – a breaking vase –
into the most ordinary sight of trees, light, water.
This see-through moon shouted that its glow would never die.
Like a scholar's work, it passed truth on, clarifying its glint.
Out in the dark, away from the fire, it was singing its songs.

•

All of these moons were moments of change and movement.
A poet never stays still, never stays in one place, you said.
Keep moving. You made it your particularity.
This is the connectedness of all your work.
It's not just that poems carry the dead's lost frames,
it's that your voice wasn't just yours, yours only in speaking,
there when needed like an implement, a tape, a tune.
It was a voice beyond voice – really, I suppose, a voice of death.
All chance encounters kept your birth still travelling.
Later you made your poems in your fibro kitchen.

There was still so much there, left for the telling.
Sure, poets are moonish things – who needs them? –
and to write absorbs all energy. It messes up living.
Poets have dogs (white spirits) which dog them all their lives.
Their thought's obsessive, singular. Like yours,
a conversation woven out of things which, not heard, sing:
a snake's unwinding movement, a bat against red sun,
a quote, a memory, a face. You got it right always when
you made that sound occur unnoticeably,
just after your listeners thought they knew: my one regret,
that, working for the radio, I never got it down.
So much light wavered across those watery tongues.
So many places caught behind a half-caught voice.
Some poems deal only with plain hard facts
of flowers and lichen, rocks along the coast,
that 1950s sense of hiking up a track, of being first
to see the inland ridges rippling out at dawn
with their blue bands still fuzzed with forest-mist.
You were a poet of eminence, echo, rain-washed air,
of places travelling from breath to transposed breath,
all of them journeying from the one who spoke
that thing which must be heard. You were of the people,
you were one of the first. Not romantic,
the work's pure document. It's clear, broken sense.
The mode was two or twenty generations old.
Back of it, the star-tribes hung in their cold dark sky
across a land tilting to its edge of aquamarine –
how strong today the sense of all the voices which you heard.
Who'd dare to do it now? But there you caught echoes audible
in all the sandbar estuaries of death and wreckage.

One morning driving back to Sydney, I turned off the road
on the way down to your place. It was nearly midday:
no daylight moon. Cicadas racketed in a windless gully –
a massed choir of them invisible in waist-high scrub.
Their dense clatter gathered a few feet above the ground,
sensitive to the way a cloud shuttered overhead.

Like dust blown in the eyes, fitful, coming, from everywhere,
they stopped suddenly, then picked up again over there,
finding the next slope, calling back from either side,
building a link like a track down which to walk,
building a hissing noise "out on the iron plain" over stones
whose edges were worn away like the edge of a sink's formica,
revealing layers like tidal marks in the sound of "nin-nin-nin,"
"living there simply in that greater solitude"
on a bank of wandering noise, "listening to the whispered speech,"
"the merciless suns," building from wing-cases, from green
hopping and hoping in the cataracts of leaves
with "the blind, brute impulse to break" out of that ruckus,
over the edge of the mirroring, tell-me-each-detail plain,
over the place where "Ejenak slept," survivor of friends,
building "the speech that silence shapes, but keeps"
a crescendo of clipping noises hushed like "deepening rain,"
"inaudible" because it gets stronger and heavier,
facing a return of a singular high-pitched player one side –
like the noise of wind in "a wild cherry," it "makes good shade –"
or, once walking with you in moonlit sea-dusk, your "Look, among the
        boughs."

A moon singing you, source of late sea-light, four years gone.

Fire

Red Wattlebirds

Coming away from the surf and the brightness
of a beach littered with blown-over bits
of she-oak, the quietness of this interior
with its balconies of palm-trees
and its ceiling-fans wobbly as the water
wavering in the yard's scalloped blue pool
is a cool repetition of stillness.
Stillness in wind and surf. Stillness here.
Stillness in the mind of someone walking
where the transparence of three-foot dumpers
collapses into swans'-wings whiteness –
matched by the stillness of the courtyard
honeyed with its half-wet, hot light blazing
against blinds and carpets. But paler there
on the balcony's wicker chairs. I've come home
to an afternoon of Rachmaninov and
Sibelius on the sound-system; to a time of
sea-clouds and ocean-light
from which the dazzle stays forever
bright as a saucepan. It's the
wattlebirds in the wind-torn banana
leaves which link up pasts and presents,
on time with dusk just starting to happen:
unstructured notes, memory-links of other dusks,
their squawks land also on a backyard
fence in Sydney, or echo like rusty
hinges through misty she-oaks round
that wintry get-away house I lived in
once, down south, near Portsea. Down there, sunsets
flamed in cinemascope. Grey ocean
peered through mist and cold. Winter dusk's rain-
and-half-snow light was full of them. Now, years later,
they're back again. They've never left. For me,
they're messengers. They arrive out of

nowhere, bringing with them the yesterdays
in which they called their clinks and clunks.
They're like angels of reminder. They slide
into any light as if into the lit-up corners
of a room, chiming their metallic
calls. No longer part of Mornington
mist and Turner dusks, these half-tropics
give them the same brightness
as the sky's blue and the resonance
of the yard's deep green leaves. They're pure edge,
or sharpness. They connect mornings
with evenings, overheard from behind so
many windows. They're doing it again
right now at the point where they land
with just enough awkwardness, just enough
flutter and grasp, so that distracted
for a few seconds, I take in the first hints
of golden sideways fire bronzing
the lowest down-hanging fronds of the
flickering palm. That fire-effect hangs there
shiny as a chalice. It's music. It's light
going under into the same bronze-blue tide
which, hours before, was falling inside each wave.

Fire

The concrete boat-ramp looks out across Myall Lake,
where a patch of water's on fire again:
bright as a childsize lens held over a leathery gum leaf
it slowly goes darker and darker,
then suddenly ochre-brown,
before the first wisp, the first thin-tongued shoot,

curls up and bursts into red glow. Spreading across from the west,
all the water takes on that raging hearth,
caught in mirrored cloud-bars and widening ripples.
Close to shore, a fish bites the surface, leaving its silver rings.
Within minutes, the light's gone lemon, while mercury water turns
to black. Winter suns end always in a flash. This one, though, now lights up

a line of darker hills for campers arriving late, coping with their kids.
Their voices drift in trees. Fireflies of torches track from tent to car.
A Toyota's rear-windows stare out a final chrome in orange air.
Someone's chopping wood. A lamp's pumped up. Beyond it.
the ridge's dark lizard-skin gets mottled with first stars,
while, quivering the surface, a last flame hovers like a burning raft.

Publisher's Note

The Kangaroo Farm was the first book by Martin Harrison that I ever read, having obtained it from Peter Riley's bookselling operation in Cambridge. Peter had known Martin when the latter was still resident in England, and moving in "Cambridge" circles – as evidenced by a small booklet published in 1980 by Andrew Crozier's Ferry Press. The book was a complete surprise: here was someone tackling landscape and nature in a robust way with a magnificent play of language. Not experimental, but a long way from what might be counted as a mainstream approach here in the UK. These literary fault-lines, such as they are, aren't quite the same in Australia, but they exist there too. I reviewed the book very favourably in *Shearsman* magazine, in one of the little round-ups that I used to do in those days. I have no pretensions to being a critic, and these were intended to note in passing those things that I thought worthy of attention, and that others ought to look out for. It transpired that Martin saw it, and was pleased.

I first met Martin in Sydney at the 2005 Sydney Writers' Festival – I'd been invited there as a translator, together with a German poet, some-what to my surprise – and the subject of a *Selected* volume came up in discussions then. This eventually became the 2008 volume, *Wild Bees*, a "new and selected", published by Shearsman Books in the UK and by the University of Western Australia Press in Perth. It was UWAP's first poetry volume and, at the time I write this, it's sad to report that the future of UWAP appears to be under threat. I hope that that situation improves.

Little appeared after *Wild Bees*, as Martin's health deteriorated – he suffered from rheumatoid arthritis and also had a heart condition – and, alas, he was to die of a heart attack at the age of only 65, in 2014. He was then in the process of putting the finishing touches to another book of poems, titled *Happiness*, which UWAP duly published the following year. It remains in print, and I hope that someone puts together a *Collected* at some point; I think Martin's work warrants the reappraisal that such a volume would bring.

Tony Frazer
April 2020

www.ingramcontent.com/pod-product-compliance
Lightning Source LLC
Chambersburg PA
CBHW020215090426
42734CB00008B/1088